The Rooster Mask

THE ROOSTER MASK

POEMS BY HENRY HART

University of Illinois Press
Urbana and Chicago

© 1998 by Henry Hart

Manufactured in the United States of America

P 5 4 3 2 1

This book is printed on acid-free paper.

Library of Congress Cataloging-in-Publication Data

Hart, Henry, 1954–

The rooster mask : poems / by Henry Hart.

p. cm.

ISBN 0–252–06692–8 (pbk. : alk. paper)

I. Title.

PS3558.A6798.R66 1998

811′.54—dc21   97-21188

CIP

For Brian, Andrew, Laura, and Rebecca

Contents

Part 1

    The Tree Ladder   3
    Directives   5
    The Rooster Mask   6
    Driving Lesson   8
    The Prisoner of Camau   9

Part 2

    The Last Visit   21
    Harvest   23
    Rowing the Ashes Out   24
    The Catamaran   25
    The Ice House Studio   26
    Alzheimer's   28
    Tai Tai   29
    Mountain Burial   31
    Easter Planting   33
    The Gray Camp   34
    The Stolen Canoe   35
    Maine Wedding   37
    The Cemetery Association Map   38
    The Map-Maker's Epiphany   39
    The Incubator   40

Part 3

    Pocahontas in Jamestown   43
    The Starving Time   45
    Dioramas of King Philip's War   47
    The Drugstore Indian   49
    Indian-Head Nickels   50
    Charleston   51
    Lincoln in Marble   52
    Pan in Winter   54
    Hell Week   55
    Exiles in Williamsburg   57
    Byrd in Antarctica   58
    Sylvia Plath on Mt. Pisgah   59
    Godot at Sylvia Plath's Grave   60
    The Martyrs' Memorial   62
    Icarus on Stone Mountain   63
    The Crash Site   64
    Mercy Kill   65

Part 4

    The Oracle of Bees   69
    Digging the Bomb Shelter   74
    The Yoghurt Shop   76
    Blood Brothers in the Winter Marina   78
    The Sap House Fire   80
    The Quarry Drowning   81
    The Farmhouse Antiques Shop   82
    The Black Mitt   83

The Midnight Hydroplane Race   84
The Hermit's Gold   85
Psoriasis   86

Notes   87

Acknowledgments

The author wishes to thank the following publications:

Agni: "The Midnight Hydroplane Race"

Beloit Poetry Journal: "The Prisoner of Camau, 1964–1969" (Chosen by Adrienne Rich for Scribner's *Best American Poetry*, 1996)

Connecticut Poetry Review: "The Black Mitt"

Cream City Review: "Tai Tai"

Graham House Review: "The Martyrs' Memorial" "Driving Lesson," "Pan in Winter," "The Gray Camp" (earlier version)

Hudson Review: "The Tree Ladder"

New Virginia Review: "Sylvia Plath on Mt. Pisgah"

New Yorker: "Directives"

Poetry: "Icarus on Stone Mountain"

Salmagundi: "Charleston," "Hell Week" (earlier versions)

Sewanee Review: "The Stolen Canoe"

Shenandoah: "The Starving Time," "Lincoln in Marble"

Southern Humanities Review: "Pocahontas in Jamestown"

Southern Review: "Byrd in Antarctica," "The Drugstore Indian," "The Cemetery Association Map"

Virginia Quarterly Review: "The Rooster Mask"

William and Mary Review: "The Last Visit," "Mountain Burial," "Rowing the Ashes Out," "The Ice House Studio," "Godot at Sylvia Plath's Grave," "The Incubator"

PART 1

The Tree Ladder

Once again I shut the back door hard
on uncles quarreling over news
of war in a distant jungle.

From the trash barrel crammed with sawed scraps
in the barn's corner, I gather
small boards abandoned by my father.

Windows in the half-built house are flames
lit by an amber sun. My mother's hand
rises from the stove like a gray wing.

Rusted nails straightened in the vise
scratch my pockets; arms ache
beneath the weight of boards.

I climb past hollow apple trees
to the tallest oak on a hill
and begin knocking at the bark.

On the last sturdy branch,
I almost laugh at the crooked spine
I have nailed up the trunk,

and listen to bells counting hours
in the distant church,
to my father calling from the door.

Wind repeats one note through copper buds.
One by one stars nail their ladders
above trees on distant hills.

I climb each star with my eye
poised on invisible rungs.
Beneath the last I falter,

knowing when I return to the house
I will still hear news of war,
my father's power saw whining in the den,

and taste the half-moon of blood
I have hammered in my thumbnail
as I wait for sleep to climb the final rung.

Directives

Having left the house where the TV wails
you must wait for the moon to sculpt the dogwood
to a statue of frost, for the crepe myrtle
to catch fire so you can light your hands,
for the chimney's rag of smoke to blind you.
You must open your mouth so that stars
freeze your tongue like snowflakes.
Now you can say you are a wind
wholly without body. You can travel
past trees bowing and shaking their flags,
past hayfields muttering simple prayers.
You can climb slopes on the Blue Ridge
and lose yourself in the dark between stars.
Now there is nothing to do but go back
to the house, nothing to do but whisper
your song of starlight and distances
to your daughter who wails in her crib,
open the window and point to red candle flames
on the dogwood, bones of pepper plants and tomatoes
bending toward cultivated loam, milkweed seeds
parachuting over garbage pails and newspapers
like words you give her to float and take root.

The Rooster Mask

In the room where my childhood ended
warheads of frost flared from panes.
A *Time* photo of Kennedy and Khrushchev
hung over a tattered map of Cuba.

The music teacher hunched over his piano,
gold tooth glinting under a hive of lights.
His black hair shone like a coffin.
His fingers chiseled at keys of ice.

He stalked the rows and demanded
I play the rooster in the Christmas play.
I taped on red wattle and comb.
Blood hung from my scalp and throat.

When I sang, words stuck in my teeth like seeds.
Rows of scrubbed faces swiveled into mirrors.
Jesus snickered beneath his halo.
Wise men lisped my name behind cardboard camels.

I studied the songbook's notes,
black flags caught in fence-wire.
Blood smoldered behind the rooster mask
until the whole room filled with smoke.

Tonight, in the school closed by referendum,
faces assemble at their desks.
I slip on the wrinkled mask
and crow my song to a child in straw.

Wind whispers one syllable through glass.
The moon pencils the courtyard's crab apple
across my desk. I trace its bloodless shadow
with a finger, thorn by crooked thorn.

Driving Lesson

We keep telling stories to make the dead come back.
I know that's him, pale wave fading into dust
that puffs as his father guns the truck toward church.

What I remember best is fall. Apples cracking
beneath the truck's slick wheels. His bronze hand
nudging mine through the gearshift's H.

The day he taught me how to drive, mourning doves
pecked salt dumped in ruts by winter trucks.
A rabbit zigzagged down the center line and froze.

Now his house is a skeleton of coal, his face
blank as moonlight on rafters in the barn,
his wave gray as webs in empty stalls.

Once I brought him maps. He marked one road
blue from Connecticut to Mississippi,
said he'd work a tugboat down to New Orleans.

Twice he drove halfway there, then drove back.
He studied new maps, colored different routes.
Heavy metal boomed from the truck he spun through dust.

That day we picked apples from his father's trees,
wind was brushwork on a snare, sun a quiet horn.
He swore he'd drive west someday and not turn back.

The Prisoner of Camau

1.

It was the rustle of nurses that brought him back,
touch of their hands that astonished.
Their voices lulled.

Officers explained his right to counsel.
He told them he starved five years in a bamboo cage
no longer than his body.

Sky fell each night through bars,
bruising like plums.
The moon pecked his mat for seeds.

Guards dragged him to a hut to sign their papers.
A radio screeched
like an orchestra of crickets.

They cut three fingers off each hand,
leaving two to hold a pen,
two to hold their papers.

He told officers he'd composed
an epic of the moon,
plotted an escape through constellations.

An officer asked about weapon dumps,
tunnels beneath the camp,
secrets he told his VC captors.

2.

When he flew to Charleston,
the moon wore a phosphor crown.
Sun smoldered all day on molten streets.

Black smoke plumed from buildings on the news.
His fingers twitched like ghosts
from snuffed wicks.

The local papers got his story wrong.
For months
he lived in a different time.

Mortars flared
in ducts above his bed.
Geysers of mud spouted from the marsh.

He woke on a cratered dike.
Shapes flapped like crows,
shouting "Mau di! Mau di! Mau di!"

They bandaged his eyes with a rag,
buried him beneath a tarp
in a sweltering boat.

A pole knocked like a broken clock.
When it stopped, a goose
squeaked in a hamlet near Camau.

3.

In the bamboo cage,
fungus etched a map
of the jungle on his thighs.

Guards bowed and smiled,
shoving fried minnows
and rice through bars.

He told himself a story
was a poultice
for shrapnel beneath the skin.

He retraced the cold canal,
the night march to the paddy,
pigs rummaging beneath the sentry.

The first bullets scooped divots
from the water's silver
as they ran toward smoking huts.

It ended with peonies of flame
on thatch, the platoon
stalking sandal-straps

through banana groves and pineapple fields,
tossing compasses into air
when mortars hit.

4.

After they wired his hands to a board
and hammered a machete through knuckles,
flinging stubs to pigs,

he lay on bamboo poles,
watching ants carry torches
of rice into soft brown bunkers.

A tree shrew entertained,
preening on a mangrove branch,
gathering fish spines for a nest.

Its claws kept time
until a guard shot it from its pole.
The moon was delirious,

scratching its skull to a gray knuckle.
He signed the guards' story
so they would unhook spotlights by his head.

He plotted stars like Scheherazade,
connected episodes of radiance and dust,
strolled through the Zodiac.

On old roads in heaven
planets gave him ideas
and maps for his journey.

5.

Unwrapping gauze from his hand,
he saw his father's ghost
in his palm's crossed life-lines.

A week before his father died
they watched a juggler
on the "Ed Sullivan Show" spinning plates.

One wobbled
like a gyroscope
and the others crashed.

His father said: "Think of it.
The man disgracing himself before millions
because he couldn't keep his plates up."

As if planets had fallen from circuits,
the galaxy teetered from its axis,
God stumbled from clouds.

He didn't question.
He hadn't been trained to question.
He had been trained to keep the plates up.

Backed against bamboo corner posts,
he saw his father weeping into the spider web
of his life-lines.

6.

When the monsoon hit,
the jungle flickered,
an old, grainy film.

He lay on a slatted mat,
braiding a noose of straw
to knot to the cage roof.

Would the rafter break?
Would a guard cut him down
with a well-placed bullet?

The moon slimmed to a fishhook.
The noose fit snug as a tie.
He began to chant the last chapter of his epic.

After guards took the rope
he built a *hacienda del sol*
night after night.

He designed every room,
every picture and plant.
In principle, it was a sundial

glued between cage walls
with the saliva of imagination,
the bric-a-brac of stars.

7.

To celebrate its completion
he scratched a baseball diamond
on the bottom of a tin cup,

marked first base,
second, third, and home,
poked a hole for a bamboo splinter.

Spinning the dial
to determine hits,
keeping score with rice grains,

he played two full seasons,
before guards claimed he prayed
to a battered chalice.

He invited them to his batting cage,
introduced them to stars:
Mantle, Williams, Cobb, Ruth.

They took front row seats
for the World Series,
razzing him through bars.

During the final game
he faced each batter
until all the stars struck out.

8.
Practicing his knuckle ball,
he saw a helicopter
scattering guards into elephant grass,

signaled to the pilot
to swoop toward the dugout
outside his *hacienda*.

He wanted to forget
like the Mekong River
sloughing brown skin in trees,

forget the candle stubs
smoking on his hands,
his name on the guards' story.

At the hospital he drew a blueprint
of his *hacienda*,
its rooms reserved for stars,

confessed ants, a tree shrew,
and an epic of the moon
had saved him,

that his father's ghost
had spoken through life-lines
about fallen plates.

9.

In Charleston,
pushing a cart
through a frigid Piggly Wiggly,

he heard a boy cry:
"That man has lobster claws."
He dropped a rice bag on his fish sticks,

wandered through the parking lot
in a haze of sweat,
unable to find his car.

That night he woke in a bamboo cage.
Fingertips crawled
like slugs over fish bones.

He reached for them,
scribbling moonlight
beneath a tree shrew's whimper.

At dawn he rowed from the Battery,
ghosts of planters
rocking on porches.

He held up his hands
until the pink and gold mansions
and his stubs were one.

PART 2

The Last Visit

Despite cyclones of black flies, Christmas trees so shaggy
they eclipse Mohawk Mountain; despite the crow squawk
of nurses jamming arthritic feet into a minicycle's clamps,

slopping more damp toast on the untouched plate; despite
carpenter ants drilling through clapboards and gnawing
kitchen paint in perfect lines around brushstrokes of DDT;

despite Chinese chestnuts breaking down to pith and sap
in two freak tornadoes, and everywhere poison ivy shaking
out oily rags; despite catbirds thrashing through gauze

tombs of blueberries until they rip threads, twigs,
and fruit; despite blue jays hammering gold crowns
of sunflowers to toothless skulls and caterwauling

at cardinals, goldfinches, and rose-breasted grossbeaks
that bow quietly over seeds; despite mice shredding ideas
for stories in his ice house studio full of rat poison—

he gazed without fuss at poplar leaves turning gray
as arsenic, puffed-up thunderheads uncoiling over hills,
their jagged tongues spitting light at trees.

Dousing his hat with citronella, he shuffled out the door,
punctuating his talk of helicopter pilots in China
with his ski-pole walker. Through lips crimped by strokes

he spoke of blades louder than tornadoes that chopped
the Cathedral of Pines that summer—a sign, he said,
to gather up and publish all his stories of China.

Half-lightened by Prozac, he hovered once more
over terraced hills, turning his year with war pilots
into plots beneath a sky the color of paper.

As storm clouds tumbled into the mountain's cliff,
three deer nosed from his Christmas trees
to root out hard green apples fallen into hay.

Their bronze bodies twitched with stars. Their eyes
burned periods in the dark. Their shadows slipped
from hoofprints as he opened the door to greet them.

Harvest

A whippoorwill's three notes lilt through glass
and a hearse crushes gravel in the graveyard.
How still the lilies lie in their black pots.

In one window, a ladder points toward angels.
Light splinters from a silver cloud.
Glass trees shake their limbs toward heaven.

In his orchard, my grandfather climbed a ladder,
his soaked shirt translucent as glass
as he swayed and picked the final apples.

At dawn, a gray pinwheel on the news
spun up the Atlantic toward the Connecticut coast.
All morning his boots drummed the cellar stairs.

Soon sparks split through fault lines
in a sky grayer than basalt. We huddled
like yellowjackets over the apple's liquor.

He waved toward books molding on a shelf
and said: "Take them." His face was gray
as surf breaking against the cellar window.

In church, basket balanced on an artificial hip,
he climbs from a ladder painted into glass,
his hand offering one last apple from the storm.

Rowing the Ashes Out

The rusted gas pump forgets to count its zeroes.
Plywood forgets the glass in the town's one store
where hunters shot the only ghost last winter.

When the spool mill failed, workers forgot their cars
in backyard woods and brooks. Now trout forget
their names, hovering beneath demolished hoods.

In a gray cabin by the lake, wind seeps through panes.
A sepia photo flaps. Gripping knotted rope
my grandfather skis six miles of ice behind a Ford.

His prize pickerel waves painted fins at salmon.
His bass, stuffed and mounted, gapes from teak.
His ten-point buck leaks stuffing from its brow.

Outside, bats pencil the sky until it blackens.
In the cove, a kingfisher dives and hoists a flame
to light the moon as I row the ashes out.

How long will it take to learn the patience of this lake?
Tossing his ash on the sandbar, I hear him say:
"Ignore the moon, its lurid dust and spectral gaze.

"Forget the trout that leaps and spits the barb.
Forget the casts that fail. Keep rolling line
toward boiling rings until the big one grips."

The Catamaran

If I stand on the dock beneath white birches
carved with so many lovers' names the bark
blisters, I can eclipse the sun with a finger,
and watch my grandfather walk on fire
that floats in splinters on the inlet's waves.

With an arthritic wrench he bolts the plywood deck
to two pontoons salvaged from the dump,
jams the flagpole in its socket, hoists
the parachute camouflaged as a tree
he bought from Army Surplus when it failed.

Girls tan to almonds on the sandbar's raft.
An osprey leans from pine as if to cheer.
Around two boulder flags he carves the sign
of infinity to prove what won the trophy
dust has tarnished on his empty shelf.

He sails through flames kindled by the lake.
When my hand tingles on its stalk, I know
his mast has toppled like a branch from wind
gusting through the mountain's notch, his face
turned blue as water on the other side of sun.

Now he leans beneath the mountain's shadow,
tugging his parachute close to ribs. The tree
above his bones sighs like rigging without a sail.
The only current seeps through buried rock, and the girls
drove south weeks ago to crush the pulp in mills.

The Ice House Studio

I raise one black glove by his window
to darken the sun's copper wires
crawling down his panes.

Only wind hoots in the stovepipe.
Hickories creak like rickety stools.
His Christmas trees wheeze through icy lungs.

A shadow hunches by mildewed books
where my grandfather lights a candle
and scribbles on a drift of papers.

Bowing in his skeletal chair,
he shuts his eyes before the smoking stove.
Windows fossilize to coal.

A chain of stars lifts the moon
over apple trees and white trails
hatchmarked by skiers on Mohawk Mountain.

Soon the moon will shrink to a tooth,
windows shiver in cracked caulk,
shingles flap like crows.

But now he leans over onionskin
smudged with errors and pencil scrawls,
his fingers black with ink.

He no longer sees me standing
half-frozen with moonlight
on the path printed by snowshoes,

or bending toward the door
to follow the small picks of his typewriter
chipping one last story from blocks of ice.

Alzheimer's

Come near my bed and let me feel your face
and hands so I can tell which one you are.
Then you can wheel me out to watch the pond.

I can't remember names. They seem to flap
like geese in V's and roost beyond the clouds
after black ice splinters across the pond.

Yesterday the nurse pushed me in a chair
through families stumbling beneath their gifts.
Outside the air grew still and barbed with frost.

It could have been the day Boxers shot
our windows out and father stuffed us deep
in sheepskin bags and galloped out of China.

You see those eggs beside the sculpted heron?
They're smaller than the eggs my father found
on his long trek through the Gobi desert.

I touched the nest, each globe of amber dust.
In one cracked shell, sun had petrified
a dinosaur's eyes to garnets.

I told the nurse to bring them back to me,
but she rolled me toward my room. I'd like to gallop
back to those perfect nights beneath the stars,

back to those birds flapping across the moon,
those dawns when you could kneel on glassy sand
and find red garnets in a nest of eggs.

Tai Tai

Tonight the sky rumbles above the roof
like her bed dragged from the room on old casters.

A dead branch falls from a backyard hemlock.
The only light in the neighborhood is a candle.

She's in the kitchen boiling puffballs in maple syrup,
waiting for bread dough to swell in the dryer.

At dinner she says her father hunts dinosaur eggs,
sells horses and Bibles to Mongolian soldiers.

A young man in Peking has just danced her into potted palms
in a posh hotel, whispering seductive lyrics.

My grandfather slaps the table to correct her story.
A candle falls, scorching his words in varnish.

My grandmother gathers plates into a small pagoda,
lifts it above the sink so it will clatter into shards.

She has already twisted her watch to different times.
Now she unplugs every cord in the kitchen

and slumps by the tiger lily pitted with mildew
beneath a bird cage whose cuttlebone flakes to ash.

My grandfather shuffles toward his ice house to correct
stories about China for a book that will never sell.

Sleet pricks his cheeks as he searches for the moon.
Tears skid across his watch that no longer ticks.

At midnight neighbors call police about an old man
wandering the frozen road without his shoes.

Mountain Burial

I expect they will come with the children's toboggan
splintered by an oak on a moonlit run through woods,
patched with fiberglass to carry logs from the winter shed.

I expect they will wrestle it up crooked stairs,
past Mexican birds no longer singing in their paint,
mirrors too dusty to trace the clock's arrows.

They will pass aureoles fallen from the Christmas cactus,
lift me from a garden of gold peacocks and blue ferns
stitched to the quilt, and strap me to the toboggan.

Outside, lily stalks scratching Chinese characters
in snow will tremble as they set me in the truckbed
beside clanging shovels and burlap sacks of sand.

At dawn we will drive to the Maine lumber town
whose store windows crack behind gray plywood,
whose post office is a teepee of charred clapboards.

We will skid past the lake of my childhood summers
where deer browse satellite dishes tusked with ice,
and, far out, shadows crouch over holes to fish.

We will shudder west over roads warped by frost
toward a mountain whose granite peak is a white flame
kindled by sun from nothing but snow.

We will rise on a logging road once trampled by oxen
that hauled chopped fir to the river for the paper mill,
and pass a cemetery of hummocks abandoned by beaver.

We will climb by red, spray-painted blazes on trunks
through snowflakes ticking on my skin like a watch
and pass crows swooping on gusts down the cliffs.

We will slip over the pond locals claim is bottomless
where the beaver hut juts from ice like a tomb
and pause on the island of blueberry scrub in the center.

My sons will dig a rectangle as long as the toboggan
in a snowdrift wind has carved into a monument
so I may curl, at last, in the place I have loved.

Easter Planting

We snickered as his Ford rattled over gravel
with a pine box stuffed with peat and Christmas trees.
Cancers of rust bloomed on his fenders.
His cheeks jiggled when he bent for hugs.

One arm swinging a bucket of wet seedlings,
the other cradling a thermos of wine,
he teetered up ruts on the logging road.
A rattlesnake sweated around his hat.

Measuring lines with uneven strides, swinging
his planter into soil still moist from frost,
he tucked hairy roots of spruce in wedges,
then kicked them so the stalks straightened.

Each spring he trimmed new shoots
and sprayed for gall or aphid. Each summer
mulched the roots with woodchips
and joked about his heart's bad valve.

One December he lugged a chainsaw over snow,
spewing chips from trees too tall to sell.
Gas in tires flared through branches
as he stumbled from the mounds.

Kneeling over brown needles, counting rings
of amber sap, I hear him kick black trunks
toward coals and curse the sleet that day
his heart burned down to a stump of ash.

The Gray Camp

For the pond's bronze flakes, the mountain's magenta slope,
the sun pitching coins against walls of pine
dated by fishermen from another century;

for spidery panes in the outhouse where a boy once sang
to prothonotary warblers darning birch with orange floss,
for mildew on rickety bunks beneath knotholes of sun;

for the mosquitoes' falsettos behind torn screens at night,
the motorboat's whine, the soft voices of uncles
steering toward the dock with hornpout and perch;

for generations of dust passing through the moon's needle
in a cracked eave, for stuffed moose and bear
eyeing salmon sketched during the Great Depression;

for lingonberry and brook trout sizzling in buttered pans,
the hand pump chugging over a soapstone sink, numb hands
at dawn opening like lilies over the smoky Glenwood;

a radio offers news of women macheteed beside African pits,
rafts weighted with families sinking off Haiti and Cuba,
the child discarded on a turnpike by the serial molester.

The Stolen Canoe

I can still see him in the cove out front
in my canoe, mist curling through his arms
so that he cast his yellow line from cloud
before he pulled it back from rings of trout.

I see him sitting on a stool by coals
at night, telling me how he dreamt of doctors
in New York sticking fingers into holes
large as quarters in his ulcered stomach.

He looked more like a mystic than a broker.
Next day I woke to water smooth as chrome
and no canoe. I radioed the nearest ranger
who promised to help me search the river.

I didn't know why Walker had stolen the boat.
Maybe he just got tired of hiking. Maybe
he fancied himself some latter-day Thoreau
who needed to paddle the river like his idol.

We flew the ranger's plane past my tower,
down little Allagash River, checking
Chamberlain and other nearby lakes.
All we found were parties inching across

water that clouds had turned to dented pewter.
We skidded toward the dam on Eagle Pond,
borrowed a canoe from the construction crew,
and banged our way through rocks in Chase rapids.

The first time I saw him he smiled and waved
his paddle. Shirt off, head back, pointing
the canoe toward us, he let the stern drift back,
then swung the bow to face the ledge's foam.

Next morning, while a cold front blew in,
we saw him on some rocks. Rain glazed his face
as if it were the sun. He smiled and hooted
like a loon before he plunged again toward foam.

At night we heard his steps in every twig
that broke in fire, his breath in every gust
that shook our tent, his voice in every owl
that flapped through moonlit pines above our heads.

At dawn he teased us toward the river's falls.
We portaged through clouds that swirled from cliffs
and looked for signs of footprints on the trail,
finding nothing but mud and slippery roots.

Below the falls, beyond my canoe's green bow
cracked in suds and moss-furred stones, beyond
gunwales and thwarts splintered between two logs,
we saw him bobbing, neck sleek and black

with down, wings flicking water from his back
as if to wave one final time, dark bill
split to taunt us before he plunged
beneath the river's sheen toward distant rocks.

Every morning I hike the mountain trail
to the fire tower, I hear his eerie cry
above the river, his wings beating wind
like my own as I climb to my dome of glass.

Maine Wedding

Fathers in red flannel jackets lean from chainsaws
that spit gold teeth from firewood, and never wave.
Children flex smudged wings on snowsuits,
chewing icicles tainted with acid rain.

The nude mannequin crossed with bandoliers
of shotgun shells under "LIVE BAIT AND AMMO,"
eyes the couple pulled by oxen on a sledge
that once hauled pulp logs down the mountain's ice.

At the church still shingle-nailed with tarpaper
from the storm that stole its only bell, loggers
clomp past pews, faces dotted with tick-bites
from shaving for the first time since November.

Ice breaks on the lake and the organ groans
through their teeth. Still they smile
at the woman preacher dropping rings, the groom
whisking snowflakes from his father's only suit.

They smile at brothers lifting groom and bride
onto a raft of chainsawed birch, and chant
Scottish ballads as the couple floats through graves
and thawing grass to docks by summer camps.

The brothers hoist a sail painted with a loon,
scatter balsam and splash in polished shoes.
They shout, "Never look back," then shout to wind
to guide them through ice toward a different season.

The Cemetery Association Map

It didn't seem right, walking on the dead all day,
digging through frozen soil for corner pins,
cutting a line through juniper and yew.

On subdivided farms, stones marked one plot's end
where deeds predicted. No brush snagged
theodolite and tribrachs in the fields.

By the cemetery gate, cows snapped rusted wire,
trampled plastic wreaths and iron crosses,
chewed apples fallen onto graves.

All day I walked the boundaries,
balanced mirrors over rusted pipes,
found whole families buried beneath single dates.

At home, the computer printed only lines and numbers.
Black ink turned the dead to rows of squares.
The final map was abstract as snow on graves.

Who knows the stories beneath the printer's lines?
Who can color each box with vivid facts
or tell how families vanished in a year?

The Map-Maker's Epiphany

He sees nothing outside but a blackened space.
For hours peepers in the swamp have pitched
their throats in eerie keys, hard-skulled moths
drummed against the squares of lamplit glass.
Hunched over a plastic table, connecting
points he measured out the day before
with theodolite and metal tape, circling
monuments that mark the ends of boundaries,
he can't tell where he is—whether he walks
through plots of Christmas trees and black-cap thorns
hooking his shins and hands, or whether he glides
like steel on ice, numbering different lots,
writing distances along the angled lines,
tracing the abstract space he knows is his.

The Incubator

My son prays all night for his baby chicken
in an incubator shaped like a flying saucer.
His prayers are experiments to test God.

When the chicken slumps he proclaims God is dead.
He doesn't want to hear the ontological proof,
the teleological proof, or sophistry about first causes.

I tell him a fairy tale about the first egg.
He stares at Froot Loops, then shuffles out the door
to cut snow-crust on the lawn into blocks for a fort.

Until dusk he lies on frozen grass,
watching angels strip their blue gowns
and hang them on trees burning in the west.

At night he has a nightmare of a gold bird
that pecks from an egg-shaped star in a black nest,
shaking blood from its beak into constellations.

Next morning, he buries the chicken in his snow fort,
fills his sketch book with flying saucers
and red galaxies wheeling to the edge of space.

PART 3

Pocahontas in Jamestown

It was the wrong day to canoe along the James.
Brittle shells of ice still clung to banks.
Clouds puffed from the power plant, radiant and deformed.

I wanted to get close enough to hear the stories
children pressed from metal boxes on the walks,
but the river scrambled words in breaking waves.

Aren't origins all the same? One tribe
killing another, then lying about the dead?
Statues never admit what lies in graves.

Pocahontas wears buckskin fringe she never wore.
Her bronze skin grows greener every year.
Pollen dusts her feathered hair to gold.

What did she think when she saw those first
shallops bob like black-backed gulls toward shore,
bearded faces muttering oaths at common shrubs?

Did she think, "Let's beat them back to sea
with thorn-tipped clubs?" Or did she lug
baskets of maize and squash to where they knelt?

Her tongue still sticks in bronze. Final answers
decay in unmarked graves around her feet.
Her story lies with bones in an English plot.

Imagine her in London. Fog and coal soot
curdling over sewers near the Belle Sauvage.
White ruff tightening around her neck like rope.

She died at Gravesend before her ship sailed home.
The eroding James sank Jamestown's fort in silt.
Fire sailed ash from roofs across the waves.

How do tourists read those voices children tease
from boxes on the walks? How do they glean
what happened from a tour guide's talk?

Her eyes point old questions at the sun.
Tarnished hands catch what answers light can give.
Wind numbs our ears with static, and we paddle home.

The Starving Time

He thought moonlight falling on hay was snow
that drifted across the dead when Jamestown starved,
wind shaking his storm door was a woman's ghost
blown from nameless graves and a roofless church.

He climbed downstairs to beat the trashcan's lid
the way he did to scare stray cats. The ghost
stared at a spider stitching wedding lace
to catch tears that fell the day they married.

Maybe she was the ghost of that other ghost,
the one who haunted the Jamestown man who quartered
his wife and cooked her in a pot, the one
who found her child buried in the river's ice.

Maybe she was the ghost of his third wife,
the one he'd brought from Boston to the farm
his fathers plowed and planted with tobacco
after the Civil War forced them into fields.

Behind columns leaning toward better times,
he rocked, recalling the day his wife refused
to eat. It was the day the doctor said
she'd deliver their child in early April.

Instead he buried her in December,
carving his own name and birthdate on a stone
behind the Presbyterian church next door.
That was when the ghost began to tap his door.

Once, dicing potatoes from his garden
into a pot of steam, he saw her eyes
glisten beneath the water. They were white
as settlers grubbing for roots and blood in snow.

He wanted to twist the gas and light the house,
but walked out and scooped dirt beside her stone,
planting the white disks of potatoes
so that she might finally eat and sleep.

Dioramas of King Philip's War

They sit in the barn before an audience of spiders.
Chisels on shelves are cold and sharp as Puritans.
Hammers slung on hooks no longer clap.

In one box a sheet keeps dust off Pokanoket braves
who have opened nine throats by a Swansea church.
In the background, clay cows trample Indian corn.

Toothpicks with green and yellow tassels
lean oddly from a papier-mâché garden.
The Indians' red paint peels from flak jackets.

Blue jay feathers droop from World War II helmets.
The church bell must be ringing beneath the steeple.
A Puritan militia gathers in the distance.

In the second box it's dark and snowing.
White threads slant into a pool of Elmer's glue.
You can hardly see Captain Church and his ragged band.

King Philip's allies huddle behind a fort
of corrugated cardboard. Red cellophane
flares above wigwams stitched from bark.

Bodies sprawl over the hard, translucent swamp.
Church carries the dead through hummocks of lichen.
It is so cold that flintlocks weld to hands.

In the third box Church kneels over different moss
by a toy soldier whose helmet is painted gold
to resemble King Philip's rumored crown.

A puddle of red paint cracks by the Indian's heart.
A sniper stands by a bush cut from sponge.
Toothpicks lean as if to lift him in their arms.

Soon his quartered limbs will turn a maple red.
Cotton Mather will pry his crow-picked jaw.
The Red King's voice will howl from every cliff.

Overhead, fluorescent bulbs buzz and flicker.
The moon hangs a skull-like crown in windows.
On balconies of rusted tools the spiders clap.

The Drugstore Indian

Pried from the dump with a pitchfork,
propped on baling wire and beer cans,
he gazed at heaven like the bankrupt farmer
mapping flies on his panes the day his cows
clattered up ramps into eighteen-wheelers.

Worms had scrolled his brow and cheek
and cut blue feathers from his headdress.
Where bronze paint flaked, his face had whitened.
I washed his soiled eyes in the back sink,
set him on the sill beside antique bottles.

All fall he stared at backhoes digging graves
in the farmer's subdivided fields,
cement trucks spinning huge eggs of slush,
wind blowing dry dirt like smoke
from distant wars to smudge the glass.

On sleepless nights, I counted hammers
banging nails into skeletons of plywood,
watched the moon shave a bow from white cedar,
arrows hiss and clatter against the roof,
cedar shingles smolder into morning.

When I woke, the Indian almost smiled
at snow burying the blond scaffolds,
reducing every ornamental bush to a ghost,
every stone wall to a tunnel, every roof
to a white goose frozen above the fields.

Indian-Head Nickels

Red skin falls from the graveyard's maples.
A couple weeps by unmown hay.
Their torch of flowers lights the planet on the hill.

At the school below, I traded coins for bolsters
with the boy who pried out rows of teeth,
grinning through his blackened stubs.

Each Indian's eye was shut on LIBERTY,
each mouth rubbed to a shallow dent,
each date buried by years of petty trades.

He stole them from his father's safe.
At home I dropped beads of Nic-a-Date acid
and watched the dates emerge from metal.

In my blue, cardboard book,
rows of gray holes filled with coins.
Gaps told the story of missing dates.

Tonight, ash falls from stars and flecks my hands.
Dust puffs from the graveyard's road.
Pines hiss above his stone, no bigger than a loaf.

Beneath the moon's worn-out, nickel face,
I open the book over the boy who split his ribs with birdshot,
and scatter the coins on his granite name.

Charleston

A slow lapping, then a gust full of salt.
A white heron stares through its shadow
printed on gold, immaculate water.
The tide withdraws, revealing its accumulations.

These could be origins: splinters of a trap
drummed by waves, a shoe floating on a runnel,
fiddler crabs dragging clubs through slime,
a broken oar wedged among bottles.

In a mirage, slaves climb from wooden graves
that have sailed all the way from Sierra Leone.
They scatter yellow teeth into furrows.
Mansions rise from their backs, brick by red brick.

Beyond the peninsula's tip built from oyster chalk,
two rivers clash, dumping their cargo of loam.
Dolphins ferry the sun from the Battery
where Henry James winced at demolished forts.

Over cannons still pointing north
a moon rises with its quiver of arrows.
In muggy streets, roaches sprint for manholes,
plunging toward the origins of the city.

Lincoln in Marble

No one shoos pigeons from his marble hair
or sandblasts tears of soot from craters
in his cheeks. No sculptor climbs a ladder
to carve or hoist his stovepipe hat.

Having stared so long at the moldy onion
of the Capitol, his eyes solidify to chalk.
His shadow slips toward fluted columns
and skies double-crossed by jets.

Stars fall into the black reflecting pool
like snow on the grave of his beloved Ann.
Again he fingers a jackknife in his pocket
while an owl hoots on a branch.

A man in torn army coat and camouflage fatigues
pushes a shopping cart full of amputated limbs
from Bull Run through Washington's mud.
Cars filibuster up Rock Creek.

Where Whitman wrote letters home for the dying,
offering them sweetcrackers and raspberries
on hospital cots of pine boughs,
grass fades like dollar bills.

Shadows touch the bronze boot
of a bandoliered soldier rubbed to gold
by NRA lobbyists, slip toward a monument
splitting green turf like a beached destroyer.

How many ghosts have read the braille
carved in its black hull? How many
have seen the dead light candles
and float them across the Potomac?

Soon tourists dressed like John Wilkes Booth
scuffle beneath Lincoln's stone boots,
trigger fingers poised on loaded cameras.
Planes reopen the wound in his head.

He stares at monumental clouds
like the time he threw away his flintlock
and stood on a stump in a cleared field
waiting like marble for the words to come.

Pan in Winter

I wanted to stay where I was.
The beech trees, even the fields
were gold. It was simpler there:
vine stalks in perfect rows
on the hill, clumps of grapes
carted to presses in the shed,
horses bowing in their stalls,
their names whispered in mist.

All fall a pileated woodpecker
practiced its drumbeat in eaves
until strychnine stunned its tongue.
My father nailed boards over holes.
Mother rocked by the fire, spinning
a story about General Hooker's cavalry
ransacking the house. In the garden
a statue of Pan exposed its cracks.

His tarnished flute had bent.
Granite horns lay in a puzzle
beneath the pedestal. Warm wind
no longer played music in the yews.
Goldfish shimmered beneath ice
like tarnished coins. I waited
for the moon to open a black door
in the pool, a shadow to guide me down.

Hell Week

There they are: black plumes
of shakos unruffled by evident wind,
dress swords glinting like ice,
white trousers and gray jackets
molded forever by the fish-eye lens.
They could be painted lead soldiers
propped on the red and white
checkerboard quad, cardboard turrets
of Camelot looming behind.

Once again my radio picks up nothing
but the static rage of hellfire preachers,
starlings heckling ghosts in Spanish moss.
Again I wake to a Norwegian wharf rat
shinnying up a drainpipe, gnawing
soap, scrawling its graffiti of slime
on tiles above the tub, chewing the nose
off the mustard bottle, scattering turds
and dark rice over kitchen counters.

Trapped behind a radiator hatch,
for three days it digs along pipes,
lighting a tunnel like a convict
with sparks from its teeth.
It eats the grain out of the oak floor
under my bed until I dream of a mouth
tunneling like the moon through glass
and spitting out stars. For three days
the exterminator refills the empty dish.

After the taped bugle plays "Taps"
I stare at the rat's eyes in the radiator
dazed with poison, call police who swear
they need a warrant to shoot, then bait
the Hav-a-Hart trap with peanut butter
and wait. That night I hear teeth
whittling bars, fur hurtling against doors
of steel, and watch the rat breathe
chloroform for an hour and keep breathing.

The next night its mate crawls
between walls, chewing toward my head.
For weeks I hear their claws
in every wind that rattles screens,
in every rifle bolt that clicks
over the parade ground's dust,
in every scuff on the quad's cement.
In the parade ground's dust, I see their eyes
burning their way through the world.

Exiles in Williamsburg

Note the courthouse stocks worn smooth
by felons, how the judge hangs her robe
on a hook in the Governor's Palace,
clinks her glass beneath wreaths of swords
and flintlock muskets, then joins the waltz.
It's a typical night in Williamsburg.

Maples drop their ruby crowns and shuffle
along Duke of Gloucester Street. Vultures
sharpen their wings to black butcher knives,
circling the dead who stroll toward taverns,
who tip tricorn hats to fiddling barmaids,
their long skirts dragging like pink peonies.

Tonight, Jefferson stands by the courthouse
and curses Hamilton's costumed Illuminati.
A mob scalds his eyes with torch smoke.
Later, he retreats to the candlelit Palace
to play a Vivaldi sonata for the judge
beneath a chandelier of glass stilettos.

Byrd in Antarctica

The last voices flared in the radio's static.
June sun thinned to blue ash on the ice cap's rim.

What was it that entered his shack dug deep in ice,
whittling bones to quills, tightening skin to a drum?

Even the cold that gelled oil in lamps
could not freeze it out.

In his sleeping bag he hallucinated wings
and woke in a damp molt.

Was it fumes leaking from the stovepipe
or just the blackness of Ross Barrier

as sunlight fizzled from the horizon
on its snuffed wick?

He heard continents of ice shift beneath him,
then nothing,

not even the clock beating its ribs.
Above, planets froze in their circuits.

The moon hardened to a sliver of ice.
Sparks scribbled a filigree around stars.

The void erupted in auroras.
Already he was flying back to Virginia,

bones light as wings, his poisonous shack
an insignificant crystal.

Sylvia Plath on Mt. Pisgah

> "I stood at the top of the ski slope on Mount
> Pisgah, looking down. I had no business to be up
> there. I had never skied before in my life."
>
> *The Bell Jar*

After snow clouds avalanched over peaks,
whiting out trail signs, maps,
and crosses on the patrolmen's jackets,

they found her body by a derrick,
face numb as an egg
in the blue folds of her parka,

cries shrill as a sparrow's.
Frost had chiseled her hands to marble,
camouflaging them among the elements.

In the lodge, faces stooped.
Questions fluttered on gray wings of steam.
A fire's gold feathers sank to ash.

In the ambulance,
she watched red strobes
slicing black trees to stumps.

Breath engraved her signature
in frost, a calligraphy
of razor-ferns on speeding glass.

Godot at Sylvia Plath's Grave

He finally showed up in a rented car,
honking at stone houses chipped by accidents,
gearbox gritting teeth.

In Heptonstall's pub,
slot machines diced for silver.
Elvis crooned from a jukebox.

A cat with Martian eyes
and fur the color of smoke,
guided him through a medieval church

whose roof was a blank sky,
whose walls had shrunk
to a petrified whale skeleton.

In the first graveyard,
the stones lay flat as mattresses
for homeless drunks.

In the second,
bodies had climbed down from crosses
and buried themselves in hay.

He stopped by a stone
and read: "Even among fierce flames
the golden lotus can be planted."

He sat in a lotus position,
uncorked a wine bottle,
broke French bread for lunch.

When he swallowed,
clouds tore their hair out,
snow littered the moors with bonedust.

Sneaking up like a grave robber,
the sun plucked the last gold petal
from the grave's rosebush,

pinched it to an ear,
then vanished forever
on a wing of flame.

The Martyrs' Memorial

They perch in stone alcoves under the cross,
their gowns blackened with soot from buses.
They like to count the pigeons by their feet.

A brass X hammered into asphalt marks the spot
where they slung bags of gunpowder around their necks.
Their faces are still mottled from the burns.

The trial continues near St. Mary's Church,
though now it's about the body and the sign,
presence and absence in the desecrated text.

On the monument's steps, kids mime their gestures,
hair spiked in orange flames against the drizzle.
Pigeons explode around their studded jackets.

They don't believe in climbing to heaven on a ladder
of sparks. They saunter past gargoyles toward the park,
gray faces expressionless as the martyrs' masks.

Icarus on Stone Mountain

All I cared for was the rush of wind,
black clouds flapping over peaks,
arcs of color in the waterfall's mist.

When frost dripped from my wing,
I swooped toward granite and ice,
the beaver lodge white as an igloo.

In the spillway's thaw,
I found the skinned body,
flesh dissolving like bread.

I built a fire by the pond,
blew the beaver's skeleton into sparks
that froze into stars.

Climbing down the slick trail,
I felt my bones shudder into bones,
pine trees scratch my skin.

For the burnt skeleton on the mountain,
the clatter of boots became my measure,
the hush of waterfalls my only song.

The Crash Site

If he closed his eyes, the plane careened toward glaciers.
The cabin skidded, tossing chips of ice.
Bad jokes coughed at night against the glass
went blank when snow avalanched from a nearby cliff.

Shivering in his lap-blanket's sweat,
he saw Coke bottles honed to scalpels,
jerky cut from corpses and baked on metal,
a dial still pointing toward the ocean.

Beneath seat cushions strapped to feet,
the snow was soft as duck feathers.
A brook cut toward a stubbly valley.
Sheep gnawed beneath a chimney's nimbus.

In the shepherd's one room that smelled of bread,
his hands thawed over a bowl of smoking wine.
His host stared at cracks in his hands
when he told his story of the mountain.

Mercy Kill

After zero nights, the fig tree froze to its root.
Pink flowers on the Christmas camellia hardened.
The box hedge bronzed and flaked. Pruning ivy
from banks, stealing rusted coins from roses,
deer crept closer, eyes luminous as amber jewels.

One April dawn, mist smoking off the river,
we gathered on the boundary, shotguns split on elbows.
Checking compasses, we strolled past Saabs
and Porsches, tennis courts stippled with acorns,
swimming pools and Jacuzzis buttoned with tarps.

The shooting began beyond the ninth-hole green.
Deer leapt through holly, collapsing like burlap
sacks into the inlet's hummocks. Wading through silt,
I knotted rope to their necks and tugged them
with the others from the river's tide.

When sun burned mist from trees, the men cracked beers
and bragged about points on antlers. That afternoon
I slept among deer gathering in the inlet's channel.
As the tide rose, they pulled me down with ropes,
eyes circling my head like a noose of amber jewels.

PART
4

The Oracle of Bees

> "What is the source of our first suffering? It lies in the fact that we hesitated to speak. It was born in the moment we accumulated silent things within us."
>
> Gaston Bachelard

1.

On the shagbark's highest fork,
a boy leans with a bamboo stick
knocking hickory nuts over the humming lines.

If only he could tap the lines.
If only he could sway among metal hives
bolted to crossed poles.

His brother waits below,
listening to voices ricochet from pole
to pole at the speed of light.

Climbing down, the boy with the stick
breaks the last branch
and kicks a stone from a yellowjackets' hive.

For three days he lies in an oracle of bees.
Welts harden on his skin.
Inside, he keeps climbing as his brother waits.

2.

In school he scribbles black lines
of mafioso crows, talons
gripped to throbbing voices.

The teacher orders him to read his story
about the last day before the world ends.
Yellowjackets drone in hives of fluorescent lights.

One by one, windows blacken into mirrors.
Wings hum around his face.
Welts redden as his classmates stare.

Walking home from the bus,
he pitches rocks at power lines,
making them groan like ice on ponds.

When bees huddle in September cold,
he pours kerosene down the oracle,
digging out combs for skunks.

3.

Beneath the barn's derelict hives
of mud wasps and white-faced hornets,
he whittles a bow from juniper,

hollows cow horns
for powder scraped from caps,
lashes tin arrowheads to stripped ash shoots.

In his tilled plot, tomatoes fatten over compost.
Pumpkin vines wander from hills of perch.
Snap peas grip their strings.

He mimics the caws of crows,
aiming tin arrows
at voices flying from the trees.

Despite chicken wire in trenches,
a woodchuck mows
his rows of lettuce down to dirt.

4.

For Halloween he puts on long black braids,
leather boots stitched with thong,
blue belt of Kmart wampum.

He smears red lightning stripes
on cheeks, slings a tomahawk
in a breech-cloth holster.

Behind St. Mary's Church
his warrior band ambushes ghosts and witches,
pillaging their sweet loot.

Sirens spin through graves.
An oracle barks
outside their tomb.

On the way home they embalm lawn-bushes,
detonate cherry bombs in mailboxes,
soap their names on neighbors' cars.

5.

In the school library, staring at etchings
of Puritans running from homes,
their shirts in flames,

at Wampanoags firing brands
into saltbox roofs
and panes black as Bibles,

he does not hear cows groaning over lit hay,
tomahawks thudding into bone,
only wind hissing through cow-scalps

on a barbed-wire fence,
a shotgun's rocksalt riddling leaves
by the farmer's pond stocked with rainbow trout,

his pointless spear whacking brush
as he runs through thorns
hooking his thigh like a rainbow trout.

6.

In church his flannel trousers itch.
His fake tie gags.
His stiff shoes squeak.

A bat-winged choir sways by the organ.
The minister sways in a white robe,
a hangman on a scaffold.

Gripping the pew, mouthing each hymn and prayer,
he closes his eyes for the night
to camouflage cornfields,

for Canonchet to scrawl battle plans in dirt
and whittle stalks into spears,
for warriors to hurl ripe ears down the furrows.

When he looks up,
the farmer waits by the barbed fence,
his shotgun raised, a moonlit cross.

7.

At home, he studies faces
smudged with grease that float
through black and white jungles on the news.

A brother brags about scalps
dangling from helmets,
ears strung like apricots around necks,

girls begging for guns in huts,
phosphorescent skulls shot from posts
for the hell of it.

That fall he climbs the shagbark
with his nutting stick one last time
to hear dead leaves rattle through heaven.

No branch breaks over the oracle of bees.
Hickory nuts scatter,
stinging the power lines into song.

Digging the Bomb Shelter

The gray scar of Cuba, white arrows stuck
to missile sites—that was the evening news.

Each morning on Quanopaug Trail, hunters loaded
shotguns and ambled from trucks in orange hats.

Their blasts ricocheted off cliffs. Grouse
and pheasants flurried toward our posted fields.

With shovel, pick, and iron bar, I scared coveys
hiding in spruce on the toboggan hill,

and dug a hole in gravel for the bomb shelter.
Leaning on roots, I studied a twisted cloud

until I saw cement walls and bunk beds underground,
the red sun mushroom over a distant hill,

leaves gust into radiant ash,
my own shadow etched on gravel.

The trout pond hissed. Skeletons engraved the mud.
A snapping turtle melted beneath its helmet.

The whole earth teetered on its axis until I stood
by a Douglas fir and heard the farmer swear Italian,

his cows drum old paths toward the barn,
udders heavy with milk for the new machines.

The Yoghurt Shop

When Mr. Thomas bought the house with his wife
I helped paint walls, tack carpet onto floors,
build a shed for tools, spade loam for spinach.
Dropping seeds in the long furrows, he said:
"Home is the only place where I can work."

His wife wrote upstairs. He fixed me tea
and cookies, sketched complicated shelves
on a napkin, touched my hand before he spoke.
Looking at the fire, he said: "You stay
with me. We'll build this house together."

One night I heard shouts. Mr. Thomas
waved on the sidewalk, face pale as cabbage
beneath the streetlight's bugs. His wife
slammed a car door. A shadow drove her up
the street and parked beside the Tollgate Inn.

Next morning he never said what happened.
We taped plastic around a window, varnished
scars on the new front door, drilled holes
in floors for radiators. That night ice split
the bathroom's pipes and a ceiling fell.

The last time I saw him was Christmas Eve.
Carols drifted in from St. John's Church.
He drank Woodpecker cider, prodded sausages
in a pan. Rather than talk about his house,
he counted stars of frost on the kitchen window.

I was too young to know what made him count.
A priest found him by the churchyard crèche,
face twisted toward a star blown out by wind.
Now his house is a yoghurt shop. A doorbell rings
and children cry for different flavors.

Parents fill their hands with colored swirls.
His widow punches numbers and counts out change
while her lover chats. I sweep the trash
from the patio mortared above his garden
where spinach seeds tap against the stones.

Blood Brothers in the Winter Marina

Deaf to sirens winding through ice,
the boys tunnel under the chain link fence.

On stepladders, they tear the green tarp
from the millionaire's yacht,

fumble with screwdrivers and screws,
unhinging his cabin doors.

They've come with cigarette lighters
to smoke his silver-tubed cigars,

with stomachs doused with milk
to swig gin from shot glasses.

Over cold stacks of girls
pulled from a mahogany cabinet

they open their jackknives.
It's been planned for millennia—

the handshakes exchanging blood,
the incantations about brothers

puffing through the cabin's mist,
glazing the portholes with frost.

The moon billows like a spinnaker.
The gold claw of the lighthouse

tugs their yacht through the harbor
toward an island of granite and ice.

And of course the black cross stalks
their mast—invisible, soundless—

and the shadow with a bullhorn,
barks orders from shore.

When they clamber on deck,
the boys are miles out to sea.

When they turn toward home,
wind freezes their knuckles to the rail.

The Sap House Fire

Black boards hunker beneath a November wind.
Foundation stones return to niches in the leaves.
The roof preserves its posture of collapse.

The iron stove squats like the old man's dog,
cast in rust. Gray birch saplings sway
like his back when he stoked the fire.

In March he drove us over sodden ruts
and snow, singing to his favorite maples:
"Sugar Maria, run wild for me this year.

"Sweet Jennifer, don't dry up like a dusty road."
A hand drill's butt in ribs, he cranked gold
spirals, then tapped spigots and hung the buckets.

When sap ran fast he catnapped by the stove,
one ear tuned to logs snapping into coals,
the other to syrup draining from the pan.

Each noon he dipped his spoon in channels
above the stove, dripped sweet amber onto snowballs
we crushed on tongues or threw at prowling dogs.

Around Easter, sirens woke us in our rooms.
Strobes reddened maples near his roof.
Flames erased the stars huddled above his hill.

Today we poke black buckets with rakes and picks,
pry out jars clumped like jellyfish over bricks,
break glass for one last trace of amber syrup.

The Quarry Drowning

All spring, china jittered on shelves.
Rockdust unfurled from dynamited hills.
After snow melted, the ground still shook.

In June we clipped the padlocked chain
hanging like a necklace between quartz posts.
Our truck shimmied over washed-out ruts.

Wind lisped through hemlocks.
Still, we stripped by the quarry's lip
and leapt into water green as beryl.

In the cliff's deep shadow,
a bulldozer rusted on its treads.
A crane jutted like a steeple.

On that high cornice
we bet who could dive to the crane's shut door,
kick rusted levers so the boom toppled.

Daryl clawed through yards of water.
His face flashed once like a sunlit minnow
over the gauges' zeroes.

The levers and boom stood still.
Small eggs of breath
wobbled to the green surface.

He never rose from his deep throne.
Cries of blue jays pinged off cliffs like chisels
and the crane still loomed over the still quarry.

The Farmhouse Antiques Shop

Isn't this where the farmer counted quarters
for my pay, cursing flies in Italian,
T-shirt mapped with continents of dung?

Isn't this antique pitchfork the one he threw
at rats gnawing seed beside a frantic cow,
this shovel the one I used to fend off horns?

Sun ignites a silver candelabra on veneer.
A fan blows air-conditioned air at hutches.
Spectrums fall from a tinkling chandelier.

Tin lanterns and china plates decorate walls
where roaches cruised for spattered food,
and a demented grandson sketched his favorite goats.

Out back, the rebuilt barn is filled with glass
and mahogany tables where I balanced wheelbarrows
over two-by-fours to the manure heap.

Now no inspectors check the vats for flies.
No pigeons claw the air over the farmer's gun.
No cows knock their yokes as feathers splash.

Where straw-flecked dung ripened until it smoked
zinnias lift gold suns from well-hoed loam.
Aromatic bark snuffs out weeds and thorns.

In the barn's far corner, a black spider
spins its lines around an antique fly,
spitting on its wings until they shine.

The Black Mitt

Web of leather, fingers stitched with yellow-
brown thong, pocket kneaded smooth
with neats-foot oil. Streaked gray at edges,
it keeps its shape after all those hits:
a scarred lobster claw, pegged up
over mildewed balls, knicked bats.
Its Stan Musial autograph frays.
In the palm's worn lines, the rites
of childhood summers: white uniforms
shuffling from diamond to dugout,
the floodlights' buzz, the peepers' whine,
butterflies before the erratic pitcher,
the chill sweat of late innings,
wooden numbers tallying the final score.

The Midnight Hydroplane Race

Every night he stares at nothing
but bats scribbling the moon.
The heart of the wood clock
beats as softly as his own.

Rolling his steel chair
toward moths dusting the porch light,
he puts a bottle to his lips
and blows a low tune across water.

By the one dock, hydroplanes
creak from trailers into waves.
Buoys wave red flags to stars.
Faces gather on the shore.

He sniffs the exhaust from prop spume,
hears motors zipping and unzipping the lake.
As always, one wave arcs before him;
the whole boat somersaults through air.

For a moment, he hangs like a puppet,
kicking between two blue worlds.
Then the moon shrinks to a clock gear
that stops because it has no space to turn.

The Hermit's Gold

Because he stammered with a German accent,
locals called him "Spy," "Closet Nazi,"
"AWOL POW from a backwoods camp in Maine."

On poplar branches, he smeared gold
butter for his juncoes. On snowdrifts,
scattered sunflowers for arthritic jays.

He shot a hole in his untarred roof
to scare the preying owl. Hung his death mask
on a post to glower at the crows.

One April, sun split his door with hatchets.
Wind shinnied down his stovepipe
and stole his milk jug full of nuggets.

Neighbors crowbarred boulders from his yard,
chainsawed boards from every wall, scrounged
for gold in his millwheel's tumbled quartz.

Swatting blackflies with a shovel,
I panned gravel when the locals left.
Gradually my hands turned gray as slush.

The only gold was in his uncaged finch,
in new leaves worming from his poplars,
in current counting change beneath his sluice.

Psoriasis

> "Whenever in my timid life I have
> shown some courage and originality it
> has been because of my skin."
> John Updike, *Self-Consciousness*

In sleep he hunched with a red quill,
scratching "i"s on his skin.
He woke to the mirror's cold indictments.

He told his dog he was walking to the ocean
to burn his skin in the crucible of dunes,
to scour its faults in the surf's salt.

That afternoon he listened to the Red Sox lose
to static on his radio, gulls drop lime on his mystery,
a chalky moon drag waves from the beach.

After mothers packed kids and umbrellas into vans,
he breaststroked through the surf's concussions,
scrambled up mussel-spiked rocks to the lighthouse.

A bronze dwarf with a lantern pointed toward stairs
and a green mermaid staring at ships and buoys
where once his grandmother lit the whale-oil lamp.

He cranked her glass dome filled with prisms,
but only the moon swivelled on the bay,
polishing the pockmarked water.

When the lighthouse roof eclipsed the moon,
stars guided the last boats toward shore,
quiet motors scrawling their names on water.

Notes

"The Prisoner of Camau": Camau is a town in the Mekong Delta region of South Vietnam. "Mau di" in Vietnamese means "hurry up."

"Tai Tai": Tai Tai was the name we called my grandmother, which in Chinese means (among other things) "grand old woman."

Illinois Poetry Series
Laurence Lieberman, Editor

History Is Your Own Heartbeat
Michael S. Harper (1971)

The Foreclosure
Richard Emil Braun (1972)

The Scrawny Sonnets and Other Narratives
Robert Bagg (1973)

The Creation Frame
Phyllis Thompson (1973)

To All Appearances: Poems New and Selected
Josephine Miles (1974)

The Black Hawk Songs
Michael Borich (1975)

Nightmare Begins Responsibility
Michael S. Harper (1975)

The Wichita Poems
Michael Van Walleghen (1975)

Images of Kin: New and Selected Poems
Michael S. Harper (1977)

Poems of the Two Worlds
Frederick Morgan (1977)

Cumberland Station
Dave Smith (1977)

Tracking
Virginia R. Terris (1977)

Riversongs
Michael Anania (1978)

On Earth as It Is
Dan Masterson (1978)

Coming to Terms
Josephine Miles (1979)

Death Mother and Other Poems
Frederick Morgan (1979)

Goshawk, Antelope
Dave Smith (1979)

Local Men
James Whitehead (1979)

Searching the Drowned Man
Sydney Lea (1980)

With Akhmatova at the Black Gates
Stephen Berg (1981)

Dream Flights
Dave Smith (1981)

More Trouble with the Obvious
Michael Van Walleghen (1981)

The American Book of the Dead
Jim Barnes (1982)

The Floating Candles
Sydney Lea (1982)

Northbook
Frederick Morgan (1982)

Collected Poems, 1930–83
Josephine Miles (1983)

The River Painter
Emily Grosholz (1984)

Healing Song for the Inner Ear
Michael S. Harper (1984)

The Passion of the Right-Angled Man
T. R. Hummer (1984)

Dear John, Dear Coltrane
Michael S. Harper (1985)

Poems from the Sangamon
John Knoepfle (1985)

In It
Stephen Berg (1986)

The Ghosts of Who We Were
Phyllis Thompson (1986)

Moon in a Mason Jar
Robert Wrigley (1986)

Lower-Class Heresy
T. R. Hummer (1987)

Poems: New and Selected
Frederick Morgan (1987)

Furnace Harbor: A Rhapsody of the North Country
Philip D. Church (1988)

Bad Girl, with Hawk
Nance Van Winckel (1988)

Blue Tango
Michael Van Walleghen (1989)

Eden
Dennis Schmitz (1989)

Waiting for Poppa at the Smithtown Diner
Peter Serchuk (1990)

Great Blue
Brendan Galvin (1990)

What My Father Believed
Robert Wrigley (1991)

Something Grazes Our Hair
S. J. Marks (1991)

Walking the Blind Dog
G. E. Murray (1992)

The Sawdust War
Jim Barnes (1992)

The God of Indeterminacy
Sandra McPherson (1993)

Off-Season at the Edge of the World
Debora Greger (1994)

Counting the Black Angels
Len Roberts (1994)

Oblivion
Stephen Berg (1995)

To Us, All Flowers Are Roses
Lorna Goodison (1995)

Honorable Amendments
Michael S. Harper (1995)

Points of Departure
Miller Williams (1995)

Dance Script with Electric Ballerina
Alice Fulton (reissue, 1996)

To the Bone: New and Selected Poems
Sydney Lea (1996)

Floating on Solitude
Dave Smith (3-volume reissue, 1996)

Bruised Paradise
Kevin Stein (1996)

Walt Whitman Bathing
David Wagoner (1996)

Rough Cut
Thomas Swiss (1997)

Paris
Jim Barnes (1997)

The Ways We Touch
Miller Williams (1997)

The Rooster Mask
Henry Hart (1998)

The Trouble-Making Finch
Len Roberts (1998)

National Poetry Series

Eroding Witness
Nathaniel Mackey (1985)
Selected by Michael S. Harper

Palladium
Alice Fulton (1986)
Selected by Mark Strand

Cities in Motion
Sylvia Moss (1987)
Selected by Derek Walcott

The Hand of God and a Few Bright Flowers
William Olsen (1988)
Selected by David Wagoner

The Great Bird of Love
Paul Zimmer (1989)
Selected by William Stafford

Stubborn
Roland Flint (1990)
Selected by Dave Smith

The Surface
Laura Mullen (1991)
Selected by C. K. Williams

The Dig
Lynn Emanuel (1992)
Selected by Gerald Stern

My Alexandria
Mark Doty (1993)
Selected by Philip Levine

The High Road to Taos
Martin Edmunds (1994)
Selected by Donald Hall

Theater of Animals
Samn Stockwell (1995)
Selected by Louise Glück

The Broken World
Marcus Cafagña (1996)
Selected by Yusef Komunyakaa

Nine Skies
A. V. Christie (1997)
Selected by Sandra McPherson

Other Poetry Volumes

Local Men and *Domains*
James Whitehead (1987)

Her Soul beneath the Bone:
Women's Poetry on Breast Cancer
Edited by Leatrice Lifshitz (1988)

Days from a Dream Almanac
Dennis Tedlock (1990)

Working Classics: Poems on Industrial Life
Edited by Peter Oresick and Nicholas Coles (1990)

Hummers, Knucklers, and Slow Curves: Contemporary Baseball Poems
Edited by Don Johnson (1991)

The Double Reckoning of Christopher Columbus
Barbara Helfgott Hyett (1992)

Selected Poems
Jean Garrigue (1992)

New and Selected Poems, 1962–92
Laurence Lieberman (1993)

The Dig and *Hotel Fiesta*
Lynn Emanuel (1994)

For a Living: The Poetry of Work
Edited by Nicholas Coles and Peter Oresick (1995)

The Tracks We Leave: Poems on Endangered Wildlife of North America
Barbara Helfgott Hyett (1996)

Peasants Wake for Fellini's *Casanova* and Other Poems
Andrea Zanzotto; edited and translated by John P. Welle and Ruth Feldman; drawings by Federico Fellini and Augusto Murer (1997)

Moon in a Mason Jar and *What My Father Believed*
Robert Wrigley (1997)

The Wild Card: Selected Poems, Early and Late
Karl Shapiro; edited by David Ignatow and Stanley Kunitz (1998)